Set yourself free and fly

a   w   a   y

A.L.

Bibliografische Information der Deutschen Nationalbibliothek: Die Deutsche Nationalbibliothek verzeichnet diese Publikation in der Deutschen Nationalbibliografie; detaillierte bibliografische Daten sind im Internet über dnb.dnb.de abrufbar.

Herstellung und Verlag: BoD – Books on Demand, Norderstedt

ISBN: 9783755753650

Covergestaltung: George Luni

Contentnote (CN): The poems "Do you ever feel like this ?"(p.36), "Trapped in this (w)hole" (p. 38) and "Freeing" (p. 42) deal with depression and suicidal thoughts.

Set yourself free

I dedicate this book to: Myself.
Congratulations, you finally did it!

and fly   a   w   a   y

Set yourself free,
spread out your wings,
all that you need
is already within

yourself.

Trust in yourself.

Set yourself free

and fly   *a*   *w*   *a*   *y*

Chapter One: (Self) Care and awareness

Set yourself free

and fly   a   w   a   y

Right now and today

Put the pressure away
you already had yesterday

and what's still there tomorrow,
push away this sorrow,

take a moment to breathe,
to think about
what you need

right now and today
and then
give it to yourself.

Set yourself free

and fly   a   w   a   y

As a matter of course

Release

this light

within

yourself,

breathe in

the wind

of peace

and health,

Set yourself free

as you water

your flowers,

look after

your soul,

just in

the same way

look after

the whole,

and fly   *a*   *w*   *a*   *y*

as your body

needs food

to stay

alive,

your soul

needs care,

needs breaks,

needs time,

Set yourself free

as your eyes

need green trees,

your lungs

need fresh air,

your mind

needs seeds

of a calm

atmosphere,

and fly   *a*   *w*   *a*   *y*

so, breathe in

the air

of positive

thoughts,

do a bit

of self care

as a matter

of course.

Set yourself free

Listen

Listen
to the beat
of your heart,

feel
the pulse
on your wrist,

tell me
which or
even if parts

of you
actually live ?

and fly   *a*   *w*   *a*   *y*

Listen

to the beat

of your heart,

feel

the pulse

on your wrist,

do you feel

how much living

you're dragging along ?

How much power,

don't you think

it's a gift ?

Set yourself free

<u>Feed yourself</u>

Feed your body
with healthy food,
feed your mind
with something good,

feed your lungs
with fresh air,
      do a bit
      of self care.

and fly   a   w   a   y

Feed your heart

with some love,

do not let

it starve,

give yourself

a treat,

      feed yourself

      with what you need.

Set yourself free

<u>Give</u>

Give yourself
the time
you need,

give your pain
the time
to decrease,

give your heart
the time
- even it's forever -
to heal,

give your broken parts
the time
to stick back together,
piece by piece.

and fly   a   w   a   y

Give yourself
the time
you need,

give your pain
the time
to decrease,

give your heart
the time
to heal,

but first of all
give yourself
the chance

to *feel.*

Set yourself free

<u>Feel</u>

First

your heart

has to feel,

before it

can start

to actually heal.

Allow it.

and fly   a   w   a   y

Chapter Two: (Self) Perception

Set yourself free

Unbreakable

How many breakdowns did you have ?

How many demons came to you tonight ?

How many people simply left ?

How unfair was your life ?

How many times broke your heart ?

How much shit are you always dragging 'long ?

How much has to come furthermore

for you to finally see how strong

you are,

'cause you're still here,

after all,

you're unbreakable.

and fly   a   w   a   y

All the cries
and all that bleeding,
all the tears you washed away,

all the fights
and all that screaming
make you unbreakable.

U n b r e a k a k a b l e, you know ?

U n
b r e a k
a b l e
!

Set yourself free

The way life works

Immediately

someone is neglected,

another is preferred,

as soon as

something happens,

another has to occur,

when

somewhere night is falling,

elsewhere the sun begins to rise,

it's like an interplay, a calling,

someone questions, another replies,

and fly   a   w   a   y

when
the traffic-light for the walkers
turns green,

then
the light for the cars turns red,
that's nothing mean,

it's just
sometimes
the way it works,

it's just
our life
with all its quirks.

<u>Destiny</u>

Sometimes things
happen unexpected and improbable,
sometimes this
life is strange,

sometimes things
happen exactly the what they should,
like we're just characters
of a script on a stage,

sometimes life feels like destiny
when there're so many fortuities
that they couldn't happen for no reason,
they fit too perfectly and are too even,

and fly   a   w   a   y

sometimes it

seems to be fortuity

and sometimes destiny,

I guess, life keeps being a mystery.

Set yourself free

Incredible art

When one single human
can take so much,
when an innocent heart
can break without a touch,

and when this broken heart
consisting of thousand single parts
can become a whole thing again
after all what was,

when a body can recover,
that was once marked with scars,
when repelling turns to accepting
and instead of hate, there is love,

and fly   a   w   a   y

then every cell of this human

must consist of incredible strength

and every cell of this human

must be a sign of true grace,

consisting of invincible beauty

when the pieces come back together, heal,

when - after all what happened -

it's again and again able to feel.

Set yourself free

and fly   a   w   a   y

Memories

Don't cry because it's over

'cause you miss the old times,

smile 'cause it was wonderful

and keep these memories in your mind

at a special place where you can find

them when you wanna look back sometimes

and don't worry, they won't get lost,

rather worry about you losing yourself in them,

make sure that you are not caught

in a cage of the past tense,

make sure that you keep living

the life now and today,

let the bad behind, keep the good in your mind

and keep going on your way.

Set yourself free

Do you ever feel like this ?

Do you ever feel so empty,
like.. you feel nothing inside ?
Everything seems so senseless,
why are you even still alive ?

Do you ever find no reason
to go on, you just exist,
and you start giving up believing,
just want to give in to it

and just go,

do you ever feel like this ?

and fly   a   w   a   y

Do you ever feel like you would rather,

like.. you simply wanna die ?

Everything just doesn't matter,

what's it about, this fucked up life ?

Do you ever find yourself

drowning more and more in it,

in this sea of darkness and hell,

just want to get out of it,

of this hole,

do you ever feel like this ?

Set yourself free

<u>Trapped in this (w)hole</u>

But you simply have no power,
you simply can not climb,
like a seed wanting to become a flower,
but never catching daylight,

and you're looking up and seeing
all the beauty and the light,
and here, below beyond a reason
to keep staying alive,

you exist, lonelier than ever,
trapped in this dark hole.

and fly   a   w   a   y

And you simply can not deal

with this emptiness inside,

you are searching for a feel,

but there is nothing since awhile,

and no one hears your wretched screaming

here on the fountains ground,

below and beyond any meaning

you seek and long for a little hope,

hoping you won't last forever

trapped in this whole.

Set yourself free

It's okay

It's okay to cry,
even you don't know why,

  don't be ashamed,
  it is not strange,
  it's nothing wrong,

it's okay to fall down
and to keep laying on the ground,

  you don't need
  to always be
  strong.

and fly   a   w   a   y

Tonight

Tonight I let the pain be the pain,
maybe tomorrow it loses some weight,
tonight I let it hurt me, let it do,
maybe if I let it, it is letting me go.

Tonight I stop suppressing what I feel,
it will help me and it's okay to cry,
this feeling, it'll never leave me completely,
but I can learn to live with it in time

and tomorrow I'll be stronger than tonight.

Set yourself free

<u>Freeing</u>

Being,

breathing,

eating,

sleeping,

ageing,

being alive.

Feeling,

bleeding,

screaming,

sleeping

(repeating),

wishing to die.

and fly   a   w   a   y

Breaking,
aching,
failing,
hurting,
burning

inside.

Seeking,
misleading,
seeking
for a meaning,
for a reason,

taking a thousand tries.

Set yourself free

Trying

and trying

and trying

and dying

and fighting

and failing a thousand times.

Raising,

reshaping,

escaping,

learning,

working

all day, all night.

and fly   a   w   a   y

Preceding,

receiving,

succeeding,

believing,

healing

is harder than decaying in this hole.

Finding,

climbing,

rising,

shining,

'til you're reaching your goal

(letting the darkness behind

and saving your soul),

Set yourself free

'til you're breathing

again

and living doesn't feel like dying,

it takes a lot, this freeing,

my friend,

but it's worth, so keep on trying.

and fly   *a*   *w*   *a*   *y*

<u>Trying</u>

Trying

never means

losing,

not trying

means losing

a chance,

an opportunity,

it all.

'Cause

and fly   *a*   *w*   *a*   *y*

if you don't try,

you already lose

more than you could ever lose

if you try,

until you try

you can not actually lose.

So, keep trying!

Set yourself free

This thing called time

There are some things in life
you don't want to accept,
for example this thing called time,
the fact you can't go back

to the time you were a child,
smoked saltstick-cigarettes,
where everything was simply fine,
easy to reach happiness,

and even you're still so young,
it already feels like farewell,
it is hard to accept that
nothing stays the same,

and fly   a   w   a   y

you wanna look back
smiling
'cause it was wonderful,

but currently
you're just crying
'cause it is over now,

see,
it couldn't have been
better than it was,

the only thing
that makes you sad
is that this is now the past,

Set yourself free

but today,

it is the same,

it can be wonderful, too,

like those old days,

quite the same way,

if you allow it to come to you.

and fly   *a*   *w*   *a*   *y*

Don't worry

Just in case you are worried about

you reaching happiness

ever again in your life,

just remember there was already a time

you worried and wondered as well

and still happiness came,

so, let me tell you like the sun

happiness will come.

Set yourself free

Being afraid I

Being afraid

is such a debilitating feeling,

it keeps you off from trying,

from doing things

and sometimes

it keeps you off

from experience something cool,

from the love of your life,

from the moments that make your life,

from happiness,

but you have to bite the bullet

and you know, that's what you should do,

but it's like biting a bullet,

it's something you simply can't do.

and fly   a   w   a   y

Fear

I hate fear

especially when it's reasonless.

You know,

some fears have reasons and are important,

but they're not this kind of fear I'm talking about.

What I'm talking about is this fear

that simply *exist*

without having a reason to exist,

but what's still there

controlling me,

haunting me,

keeping me off

from breaking free.

Set yourself free

<u>Tomorrow</u>

There are these thoughts
crossing through your mind,
making you unable to sleep,

and, guess so, if you
are sleeping, they would
haunt you in your dreams,

there are these thoughts
of how the next day
could be, could end up,

there is fear, there are doubts,
time keeps running,
no way out,

and fly   a   w   a   y

you don't want
it to happen, you rather
want to skip this day,

but time keeps running
and you still haven't
found a hiding place,

it's like you're driving
an old car
and going all too fast

and you simply can't slow down,
are driving
anywhere but home,

Set yourself free

sometimes you have

to make it through,

that's something you can't change,

but did you know,

you already survived

every fucking day,

also the days

that didn't let you sleep

like now,

it's just the same

and you can make

it through somehow,

and fly   a   w   a   y

and tomorrow

will be over,

in 24 hours, alike

every day,

it's limited,

your car will keep its drive,

every tomorrow

will become a today

and today'll become yesterday,

you can survive it,

you will survive it,

at least you survive

in some way.

Set yourself free

and fly   a   w   a   y

Chapter Three: (Self) Liberation

Set yourself free

Never stop doing what makes you happy

Be passionate
about the things
igniting a fire in your heart

if it burns away
things going wrong now
and what's falling apart,

enjoy and smile at
the smallest things,
sometimes they're all that remains,

hold on to what makes
you feel the living
that is pumped through your veins,

and fly   a   w   a   y

do more of what

makes you forget

what tomorrow might be,

keep doing crazy stuff

if it's the reason why

for a moment your sorrow's set free,

keep falling in love

if it's a love that fills your

tummy with butterflies,

keep laughing about childish jokes

if it takes away mountains of your heart

that would crush it otherwise!

Set yourself free

There is no need
to mind the ones
deriding, smiling at you,

there is no need
to stop doing
what does *your heart* good, dude,

I mean,

why ?

and fly   a   w   a   y

Just because others

are too genteel

      for what *your heart'*s

           beating so fast ?

If it makes *your life*

a bit more worth of living,

      then, the fuck, do it,

           at least for your heart!

Set yourself free

and fly   a   w   a   y

If you're happy

„ *You are happy.* ",

says your heart,

but no one thinks you should feel like that,

so they make you

feel insecure

about your own happiness,

Set yourself free

you're allowed to feel happy,

     I mean,

     it doesn't have to be perfect

to feel happy

     and in general

     doesn't everyone have

     to define

     their unique,

their own happiness ?

and fly   a   w   a   y

There is no battle,

no *wrong* way,

there is no *better* or *the best*.

The only thing

that counts

is the feeling in your chest

and all the things

around

shouldn't oppress

this happiness.

Set yourself free

,, *You are happy.* ",

      says your heart,

      but no one thinks you should feel like that,

      so they make you

      feel insecure

              about your own happiness,

and fly   a   w   a   y

„ *You are happy.* ",

        says your heart,

        and you deserve this happiness,

        if you are happy,

        it's what you are,

                don't listen to the rest.

Set yourself free

Standing still

I feel like
I'm not allowed
to stand still

even for a blink of an eye,

to just breathe,
close my eyes
and lie down for a while,

and fly   *a*   *w*   *a*   *y*

'cause I feel like

if I do it,

then the world

would outpace me,

I unlearned

to live in the moment,

the here and now,

                  I can't pretend I am free,

Set yourself free

the world
pulls me further
and if I breast,

it pulls ahead so fast,

then I've to race
to keep pace
with the world,
to not be the last,

to not lose the connection

'cause I feel like
I'm not allowed
to stand still

and fly   a   w   a   y

even for a second.

Set yourself free

Looking up at the stars

How about turning off these voices
and looking up at the stars ?
Without any worrying about
what will be, is or was ?

It seems to be a science
to be able to be silent,
it seems to be real art,

not making a sound,
slowing down
in a world so loud and fast.

and fly   a   w   a   y

How about starting to dream big
again believing in shooting stars ?
To make our world a little more magical
rather than trying to understand it all.

When did and why did we even stop
turning our confused and fanciful thoughts off ?
If they make our world so colourful rather than blue.

Where did we lose our faith ?
Who said it'd be impossible or even too late
to make our dreams come true ?

Set yourself free

How about turning off these voices
and looking up at the stars again ?
How about all we take is the moment
and each other's hand ?

If nothing lasts,

why do we want it all ?

The here and now is our real gift,

and if you ask me,

I'd rather be

in your arms than own all that exists.

and fly   a   w   a   y

Living the moment

Life is happening right now
and what, tell me, matters there ?
In this moment, in this heartbeat,
right in this breath of air ?

Nothing else, but the fact
that you're here with me,
so, empty your mind, it's full of crap,
            just do it, darling, set it free!

Set yourself free

<u>Keep calm</u>

Life is no race,
life is not about your aims,
life is everything, but what
everyone pretends,

don't stress yourself,
life's not about achieving your aims,
it's more about the path
that leads to them.

and fly   a   w   a   y

Happiness can be found

Happiness can be found

in a hot cup of good tea

or in the singing of birds,

in the rustling of autumn leaves,

happiness can be found

when we truly search for it,

stop thinking 'bout what's missing to feel happy,

but what's worth to feel like this,

happiness can be found

in the small, the simple things that we

might take for granted, overlook

while we long for something greater to reach.

Barrage

Something's keeping me
from being who I really want to be
instead of never changing,

my heart from letting go
of what I shouldn't hold on to any more,
even I know this ends with heart-breaking,

myself from living the moment
and from closing the past's door,
my mind from worrying about the future
and too often looking back to what was,

and fly   a   w   a   y

something's keeping this little bird
from getting what he actually deserves,
from freeing himself and flying away,
freeing himself and following his way.

Set yourself free

Old thought patterns

Anyway, almost nothing lasts forever,
one day almost everything will shatter,
so why shouldn't our thought patterns
that keep us from the things that matter,

from living our lives,
from dreaming our dreams,
from leaving things behind
and allowing new things,

let's set up our mindset
and make it feel upset,
'til we reach a healthy mindset
and save us from ourselves.

and fly   a   w   a   y

Unflashy bird

There is this unflashy bird

making his way,

he doesn't seem like a bird

with a lot to offer,

withal there is so much he could show,

so much being comprised in himself,

that he simply doesn't extravert,

he drags it with him like a coffer,

there is so much more behind a person's face,

so much more under a bird's wing,

there is so much love in the quietest heart

that needs to be tickled of within.

Set yourself free

There is this unflashy bird
carrying this fire inside,
but somehow he won't
let it go outside,

it doesn't have to be fear,
I don't think he's very afraid,
maybe he's just waiting for the right moment
till it is too late,

maybe the other birds simply
take his space,
so he doesn't get an opportunity
to express himself.

and fly   *a*   *w*   *a*   *y*

Set yourself free

The moon, the stars and myself

I'm sitting in silence
watching the moon and the stars,
they feel so close while this
earth feels so far

away,

in time somehow
everyone left me apart,
alone, on the ground on the side
of their boulevard,

but that's okay,

and fly   a   w   a   y

'cause it sets me free,

but also tears me apart,

when there's no one but me,

I feel so worthless, it hurts my heart,

makes me bleed,

but it's also a kind of freedom

I've never felt,

when no one cares, then I can do

what I always wanted to make

and be who I wanna be.

Set yourself free

I'm walking in silence
beside the moon and the stars,
I talk to them and to me
and I empty my heart

finally and

people's voices are slowly
losing their meaning to me,
I've got nature and most importantly
I've got me,

myself, finally again,

and fly   a   w   a   y

the chaos in my mind
is slowly going away,
it is free of memories and thoughts
not worth to save,

I create new space,

nobody knows where I am,
me neither,
but I know this path
will make my demons weaker

'cause they see I can.

Set yourself free

Maybe I'll come back
when I find what I search
for peace, feeling home and esteeming my worth,

when I find myself
and I find out
that I can do anything on my own,

that I'm the person I spend my whole life
with, when myself becomes a friend of mine
and I'm satisfied,

I'll come back
when I find what I search,
I'm coming back to you,
but first I have to put myself first.

and fly   a   w   a   y

I close my eyes,

I can't see the moon and the stars,

but somehow I feel them

right in my heart,

by my side,

as the sun comes back from her absence,

back from her trip,

I'm glad to see her, but she's nothing

I particularly missed

at night,

Set yourself free

and that's when I realized,
I've finally reached the point
when myself is what
myself needs the most,

that's something I've never
thought of to seek,
but the most valuable
and desirable thing,

actually.

and fly   a   w   a   y

Listening to my heart

Listening to my heart
was one of the best things
I could do,

at first it was hard
to understand its words
and to see through,

until I stopped looking for any *words*
and started listening to its beatings,
until I realized its language
consists of *feelings*.

Set yourself free

<u>Learn to fly</u>

Taking a run,
jumping off a brink,
learning to fly
with a couple of things
is quite hard.

Releasing all those
bags full of thoughts,
feeling freer than
ever before,
now it's easy to fly away
with a lighter heart.

and fly   a   w   a   y

Taking the good,

leaving the bad things behind,

coming home

with a refreshed mind

full of strength.

Feeling exchanged,

like newly born,

like a new life is breaking

and not just a new dawn,

now it's easier to restart

and to begin again.

Trust the wind,

learn to fly!

Set yourself free

Perception

It's all about how we look at the sky,

if we call it darkness or if we call it ocean of stars,

'cause the wisest humans would value the light

and the shadow as equal parts.

'Cause, in fact, they can't exist on their own.

and fly   a   w   a   y

Untitled I

Where does this pressure come from ?

There is really no need,

you are doing quite fine,

actually.

Set yourself free

Daydreamer and night thinker

I love being a daydreamer, and I love being a night thinker; I appreciate that I'm able to hide myself in my mind whenever I'm somewhere I rather don't want to be, I'm having a deep talk with the moon and the stars while others are asleep; I am able to enter worlds that some people don't even know exist, I am able to get lost in my thoughts when things around me become too much; I love being a daydreamer, they say stop dreaming and start living your life, but I love the way I live it, how dreaming is what I'm wasting with my time.

and fly   a   w   a   y

<u>Untitled II</u>

I'm barely

hanging on,

trying to deal with

my feelings,

turning my thoughts

into a song,

'cause in this

I found my healing.

Words and music.

Set yourself free

My way of healing

I wrote songs
to make others
feel better, feel good,
feel valid and understood,
feel enough and not alone,
like they are not the only ones,

I realized
writing songs
is balm for my mental health,
as I realized I wrote them
for myself
as well,

and fly   a   w   a   y

as I realized it,

I thought I'd keep writing

not just for everyone else, but for myself too,

I didn't realize

I've already done it all the times

I've written before when I thought

I was writing for you.

Set yourself free

Music

I feel freedom
and all my demons
are pushed away by the strength
that fills living in my veins,

right at this moment
when I don't care if I'm broken
'cause I just feel so alive,
my chest is filled with light,

it's something they can't take away
that just makes me feel so okay,

and fly   a   w   a   y

music's my passion
and the way it makes me feel,
I use it as a weapon
and I use it as a shield.

Set yourself free

<u>Being afraid II</u>

I can't resent you

for being so afraid

that your mind

is so full of worries

about what will come

that you unlearn to live

the moment currently

going on.

I can't resent you

for being so afraid

in such a world

full of worries

and you don't know what to do,

I can't blame you

for being afraid,

I'm too.

and fly   *a*   *w*   *a*   *y*

<u>Don't</u>

But don't let worries
control your life,
choke your heart
and kill your vibes,

but don't let people
steal your joy,
scare your soul
and turn it cold.

Set yourself free

<u>Do (it)</u>

Your life,

you've just got one,

don't let too much

remain undone,

you have got dreams,

so, so many,

you can't even count,

but unfortunately

not endless

time, so, go,

for real,

try to make them real!

and fly   a   w   a   y

Set yourself free

Today

Imagine today
without tomorrow
and without yesterday,
just imagine *now*,

and feel the weight
being lifted from your heart
when you stop thinking about

what will be
and what was,
the future
and the past,

and fly   *a*   w   *a*   *y*

of course,

it is important,

of course,

you've to think about it,

but it's enough

to keep them in mind

instead of letting them

kill today's time,

the past is written

and can't be changed,

tomorrow can wait,

but, darling, not today.

Set yourself free

Break free

When things get too much
and you too busy
that there is no more
time left for living,

when relationships
constrain your heart
that they don't feel like a gain,
rather like a force,

when your mind fucks you up
'cause it is so afraid
that there's no more
chance or risk you'd take,

and fly   a   w   a   y

when your life is determined
by this stuff all along
that keep you from
the life you wish, you want,

from joy and happiness,
living and fun,
ease and time to rest,
from late-night-calls 'til dawn,

from achieving your dreams,
good food and good songs,
then it's time to break free
'cause something is wrong.

Set yourself free

Decisions

Certain decisions
in your life
make you so afraid,

pressure from family,
society, the whole environment,
even friends,

but you know ?
Do you know
how many people
have changed their minds ?

But the thing is,
their first decision
wasn't wrong,
it's just alright,

and fly   a   w   a   y

if first you

have to figure out

what you want to do,

it's all alright,

actually there is

nothing to lose,

what important is

you become happy

one day,

and happiness

can be achieved by detours

as well as straight away,

115

Set yourself free

so many people

changed their minds,

you would not be the first,

just give it a try,

and what of it,

if a dream bursts

or it turns out to be the worst ?

So many people

changed their minds,

but do you know ?

Most of them

are happy now

and that's the only thing that matters.

and fly   a   w   a   y

Her happiness

And there she is,

creating her own happiness

detached from everything

and everyone,

despite everything -

and everything she wanted

to become

she tried to become

and so she became,

even though

she was afraid,

and here she is,

you know, she *is* -

she doesn't just exist -

she *lives*.

Her Perception I

And there she is,

happier than he is,

not 'cause she has

more, no,

but because of the way

she thinks about

what she owns.

and fly   a   w   a   y

Her perception II

Actually,

she owns half as much

as he does,

but she feels like

holding the whole world

in her hands

'cause it's about perception

and not about what

they actually have.

Set yourself free

By yourself, for yourself

If you need love,

then give love

to yourself,

if you need to cry,

then place yourself

in the pouring rain,

if you need warmth,

then take a walk

and meet the sun,

and fly   a   w   a   y

sometimes you feel like

you need something

and you're waiting for it to come

in your life,

but most of the time

you are able to obtain

it by yourself.

Set yourself free

Up to you

But in the end

and to conclude

it's in your hands,

it's up to you.

and fly   a   w   a   y

My own happiness

And as I danced

to my own song,

I realized I can be happy

on my own.

Set yourself free

Setting myself free

And as I found

what sets my soul free,

what ignites a

firework inside,

after I almost forgot

how it feels

to feel

so alive,

I picked up my parts

off the street

I lost during all

these nights

and fly   a   w   a   y

and created

a masterpiece

and again my heart

became mine.

I set myself free

and with that

I overshadowed

every existing light.

Set yourself free

And now

126

and fly   a   w   a   y

fly away,
jump off the ground,
don't be afraid,
you will get home,

you will!

Trust me.

(You're already on your way)

Set yourself free

Set yourself free

and fly   a w   a   y

and   fly   a w   a   y

(I'm telling you, don't hesitate!)

Set yourself free

Dear reader,

what to say at the end of a book ?

In fact, what to say at the end of my very first published book ?

I just feel like I've already put so many thoughts and feelings into these poems, so I kind of ran out of words. I still have so much to say and yet I am speechless. Something you don't usually hear from a person who writes. :D

I already wrote this book about four years ago, so I can't even tell you why exactly I started writing it. But I like it. Still. I like the way I think in this book. :)

I hope that doesn't sound weird.

I just don't know what to write.

and fly   *a*   *w*   *a*   *y*

Anyway, I really hope that you actually believe me when I say that I'm honestly so happy about and thankful for you taking the time and reading my book. I highly, *highly*, *HIGHLY* appreciate that, really! :) It just makes me smile and warms my heart to imagine people holding this book in their hands and reading my words. Honestly, I can't wait to publish more books. :D

So, again and again: Thank you! :)

And last but not least: Thank you, Luni, for creating this lovely, wonderful cover! I think it's adorable. <3

Lots of love to you!
Amanda Lou

Set yourself free

and fly   a   w   a   y

Index